EARTH DAY, EVERY DAY

EARTH DAY, EVERY DAY

TOM J. ERVIN

Palmetto Publishing Group
Charleston, SC

Earth Day, Every Day
Copyright © 2020 by Tom J. Ervin

First Edition

Printed in the United States

ISBN-13: 978-1-64111-757-9
ISBN-10: 1-64111-757-5

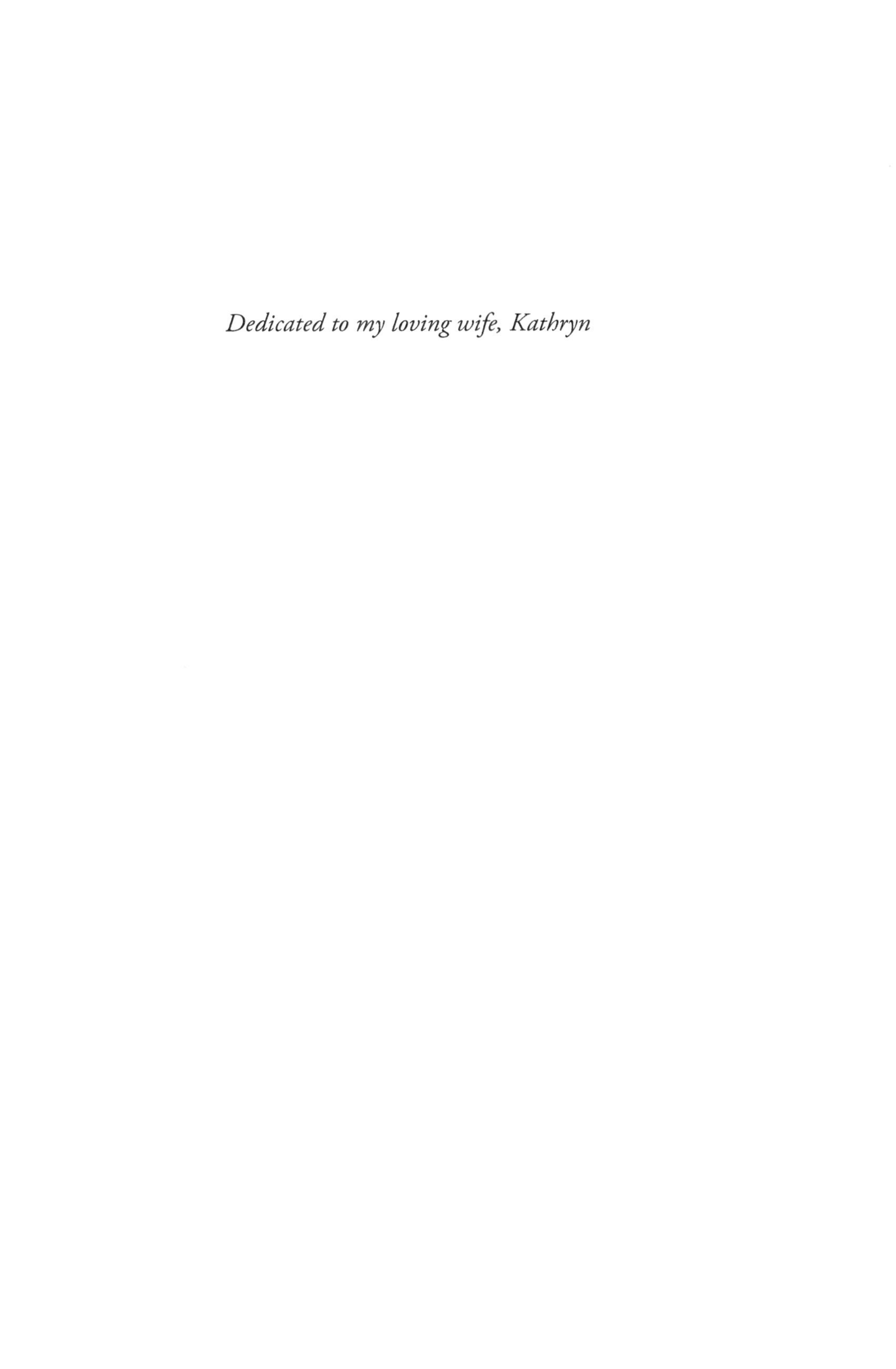

Dedicated to my loving wife, Kathryn

TABLE OF CONTENTS:

Section One:
The Global Challenge:

Chapter 1:

INTRODUCTION

Defining Climate Change and Global Warming

While the terms *global warming* and *climate change* are often used synonymously, it is important to understand the difference. *Global warming* is caused by the increase in greenhouse gas emissions that get trapped in Earth's upper atmosphere, causing heat to become trapped (1). *Greenhouse gases* include carbon dioxide, methane, nitrous oxides, and chlorofluorocarbons (CFSs). These gases absorb heat energy emitted from Earth's surface and then radiate it back, warming the Earth's surface. This is sometimes referred to as the *greenhouse effect.*

The Industrial Revolution brought an increase in greenhouse gases as more wood, coal, oil, and natural gases were burned. The automobile brought more harmful emissions, with the combustion engine. Today, natural gas fracturing, or fracking, has released more harmful methane gas into the atmosphere. *Climate change* is the term used to describe the overall harmful man-made impacts on the Earth's climate (2).

There is more carbon dioxide in the atmosphere today than there has been in almost three million years (3). Extreme weather and natural disasters are worsening as a result of our changing climate. These extreme weather patterns bring more frequent tornadoes, wildfires, hurricanes, severe thunderstorms, floods, and even droughts. With worsening conditions, the air has become drier and warmer, increasing the risk of natural disasters like deadly wildfires, such as those that have recently occurred in California, Brazil, and Australia.

Even though there is overwhelming scientific evidence to confirm the existence of global warming, some are still in denial about the fact that the Earth is warming due to increased man-made pollution. The Kaiser Family Foundation conducted a study in 2019 that found that about eight out of ten Americans believe that human activity is fueling climate change (4). Roughly half believe that urgent action is needed within the next decade if humanity hopes to avert the worst effects of climate change.

The Earth Stands "On the Brink of Failure"

In 2019, the *Oxford Dictionary* chose "climate emergency" as the phrase of the year. It is defined as "a situation in which urgent action is required to reduce or halt climate change and avoid potentially irreversible environmental damage resulting from it" (5). Those who consider climate change as catastrophic, irreversible, or rapid now refer to it as a "climate crisis." In 2019, a poll of the US population found that 64 percent find that climate change is a "crisis" or a "serious problem," with 44 percent saying that human activity was a significant contributor (6). The most impactful human cause of global warming has been due to greenhouse gas emissions like carbon dioxide, methane gas, and nitrous oxide.

The Fifth Assessment Report of the Intergovernmental Panel on Climate Change (IPCC) found it "extremely likely that human influence has been the dominant cause of the observed warming since the mid-20th century" (7). Climate model projections indicate that twenty-first century global surface temperatures are likely to rise even further. In a moderate scenario, the likely range is from 0.3° to 1.7°C. In an extreme scenario, the temperature could rise from 2.6° to 4.8°C (4.7° to 8.6°F), depending on the future rate of greenhouse gas emissions and on climate feedback effects. These findings have been recognized by the national science academies of the major industrialized nations and are not disputed by any scientific body with international standing.

The Earth's average temperature has increased by about 2°F during the twentieth century, according to NASA (8). That might not sound too bad. However, based on Earth's climate record found in tree rings, coral reefs, ice cores, and fossils, the scientific evidence is clear that even small changes in Earth's temperature can lead to dramatic changes in our environment. The vast majority of scientists who follow global warming are certain that temperatures will continue to rise due to the large amount of greenhouse gases being released into the atmosphere.

"NAVIGATING THE FUTURE"

Chris Mooney and Brady Dennis, *Washington Post* journalists, sounded the alarm in October 2018 about what might happen if the world failed to address the coming climate crisis. "Nations will need to take 'unprecedented' actions to cut their carbon emissions over the next decade," Mooney and Dennis warned, while noting that the United States is the world's second-largest emitter of carbon dioxide, trailing only China (9).

The 2015 Paris Agreement concluded that the world has about a decade to meet the goal of limiting further global warming by 1.5°C (2.7°F). The United Nations IPCC wrote: "There is no documented historic precedent" for the sweeping changes that need to occur in energy production, transportation, and agricultural practices to slow down the adverse consequences of global warming (10).

The 2019 Madrid Conference dashed hope with disappointment as the world's developed nations failed to reach any agreement on how to proceed. Absent some miraculous consensus among nations, the world's annual carbon emissions are on a glide path to exceed forty billion tons per year (11). As of 2018, global emissions were still on the rise.

To complicate the math, the world's population is predicted to increase by more than two billion by 2050. Technological advancements in carbon capture and battery storage would need to ramp up on a massive scale to make much of a difference.

China is still the world's leading emitter, at 10.15 billion tons of carbon dioxide per year, followed by the United States, India, Russia, and Japan (12). The United States deserves some credit for reducing emissions by 14 percent from 2005 to 2017 (13). Unfortunately, increased global emissions negated all US progress because of a 21 percent increase in other countries' output during the same time period.

Meanwhile, glaciers in Antarctica and Greenland are melting at a historic pace, resulting in rising sea levels, which place coastal communities around the world at great risk. The Arctic Ocean could soon see ice-free summers due to the extreme pace of global warming. In February 2020, a gigantic iceberg broke off Antarctica's western coast. The Pine Island Glacier and Thwaites Glacier form the gateway to a massive amount of ice that "would raise sea levels by four feet if it were all to spill into the sea," according to Madeleine Stone with *National Geographic* (14). The recent heat wave in February 2020 melted 20 percent of Antarctica's snow cover in just a few days, leaving melted ponds of water sitting on top of the ice sheets.

Chapter 2:

IMPACTS OF THE CLIMATE CRISIS

The Year 2019 Was the Second-Hottest on Record

According to the National Oceanic and Atmospheric Administration, 2019 was the second-hottest year on record for Planet Earth (15). Nine of the ten warmest years on record were during the last decade. Earth saw its warmest month on record in January of 2020 (16); the monitoring group Copernicus also agrees that January was the warmest month globally on record. Records were shattered in Europe and Asia. On February 6, 2020, Antarctica hit a record 65°F (18.3°C) at the Esperanza Base along Antarctica's Trinity Peninsula (17). This reading is 40° to 50° above normal for this time of year and is the continent's highest measured temperature in history. On February 9, 2020, a weather research station on Seymore Island in the Antarctic Peninsula registered a temperature of 69.3°F (20.75°C). The Antarctic Peninsula, which is the part of the continent closest to South America, has been one of the fastest-warming regions in the world. This record warmth from February 6 to February 13 was enhanced by a dome of high pressure, which hovered over the southern tip of South America along with warmer-than-average sea surface temperatures, according to Andrew Freedman with the *Washington Post* (17). There was also an absence of a band of winds called the Southern Hemisphere Westerlies, which normally blows between the continents, protecting Antarctica from the milder air to the north. These high-temperature records were also boosted by downsloping winds called foehn winds, which cause air to compress and temperatures to increase. Andrew Freedman reported that the "Antarctic heat wave melted 20% of the snow cover in days, causing melt ponds to proliferate" in the *Washington Post* on February 24, 2020.

During the past fifty years, temperatures there have increased 5° in response to Earth's rapidly warming climate. About 87 percent of the glaciers along the west coast of the Antarctic have retreated during this time frame (18). Cracks in the Pine Island Glacier have become visibly wider, according to NASA's satellite imagery (19). Most of the glaciers in that region are retreating rapidly. According to a 2018 study, ice-shelf collapse and the acceleration of glacier movement into the sea at the Antarctic caused an increase of twenty-five billion metric tons of ice loss per year in the region between 1992 and 2017. Researchers are now focusing on concerns about ice loss around the entire continent. For years, climate scientists have struggled to calculate the amount of methane that is trapped under the ice at the North and South Poles.

A study published in *Nature Communications* predicts that somewhere between 80 to 480 gigatons of methane could be released into the Earth's atmosphere. All cattle and domestic animals in the world produce only.08 gigatons of methane each year (20).

Climate Change Is Real and Is Largely Man Made, as Supported by Undeniable Scientific Facts

Ninety-seven percent of the world's scientific community agrees that climate change is real and caused by man, including such agencies as NASA, the National Academy of Sciences, the National Oceanic and Atmospheric Administration, the Department of Defense, and the UN's IPCC (21). Even fossil fuel companies like Exxon Mobil have acknowledged that climate change is a real and present danger.

Climate Change Could Make Many of Our Favorite Foods and Wines Disappear over Time

Food production will be adversely affected by climate change. According to the Organization for Economic Co-operation and Development (OECD), "Climate change could worsen the prevalence of hunger through direct negative effects on production and indirect impacts on purchasing powers" (22). According to the USDFA, one in ten Americans are already considered "food insecure," meaning that there are times during the year when this population does not have enough money to purchase the food they need (23). Future food-price shocks may result from the degradation of farmland due to poor agricultural practices, coupled with the growing world population.

Even the banana is fighting to surpass climate change. The popular Cavendish banana is under attack by a disease called Tropical Race 4, which enters the banana tree's vascular system, limiting its ability to absorb water and nutrients from the soil (24). Scientists have confirmed that the warming temperatures where these bananas are grown has exacerbated the spread of Tropical Race 4.

Avocados and chickpeas have been adversely affected by severe droughts caused by global warming. Extended droughts have also impacted the peanut crop in the southeastern United States. Peanuts may be gone by 2030 (25). Grape vineyards are at risk for the same reason. Many grape varieties used for wine production are already under stress from the changing climate. Maple trees need freezing nights followed by warm days to produce maple syrup. Chocolate has been another victim of severe droughts, to the point that it could be gone by 2050. Oranges are being attacked by the citrus greening disease in Florida. Once a citrus tree is infected, there is no known cure for the greening disease. Honeybees are at great risk due to colony collapse disorder. Since honeybees are pollinators, their decline adversely affects agricultural production. Bumblebee populations are also at risk due to their inability to adapt to extreme heat.

Many of the foods we enjoy, like chocolate desserts and crackers, are at greater risk due to climate change, as some ingredients in these foods come from raw materials from West Africa. Cocoa, used in many candies and desserts, is imported from Ghana and the Ivory Coast (26). Global warming has negatively impacted rainfall in this region, dealing a severe blow to cocoa farming. Wheat crackers are at risk due to damage done to the wheat crops by extremely high temperatures. Not only will this have a negative impact on food production, but it also creates food insecurity for the local populations who need agricultural sustainability to survive.

The World Health Organization has warned that children are most at risk for experiencing food insecurity due to climate change. Child malnutrition in children is a growing concern, as food prices are predicted to increase as certain food sources become scarce. *The Lancet*, a respected medical journal, predicts that if carbon emissions continue to rise, a child born today could be living in a world with an average temperature that is 7.2°F (4°C) warmer by the time they reach their seventy-first birthday (27).

North Atlantic Hurricanes Are Becoming More Frequent and More Intense with Warming

The Carolinas are prime examples of how many southeastern states have felt the effects of global warming. From 2016 through 2019, North Carolina experienced two devastating hurricanes. Hurricanes Matthew and Florence took the lives of seventy-nine North Carolinians and caused $17 billion in property damage just from Hurricane Florence (28, 29). North Carolina experienced extensive flooding, which damaged crops, washed out roads and bridges, caused mudslides, and impacted tourism with a shortened ski season. Climatologists predict that hurricanes and tropical storms are expected to be more damaging as global warning accelerates.

Scientists now believe wind shear may have acted as a "speed bump," creating an invisible buffer along the southeastern coastline during Hurricane Matthew in 2016 as strong winds moved in the opposite direction from the storm (30). However, scientists are not counting on wind shear to offer protection from future hurricanes because increasing water and air temperatures are bringing more severe storms further north as warmer water reaches higher latitudes.

Hurricane Dorian, a life-threatening category 5 storm, hovered over the Bahamas for days in August of 2019, causing catastrophic loss of life and property damage. Dorian was the second-strongest Atlantic hurricane on record. Climatologists attribute these more severe hurricanes to the fact that the Earth's warmer atmosphere is trapping more water vapor. Atmospheric research scientists with NOAA's National Center for Environmental Information have confirmed a 7 percent increase in water vapor for every degree of Celsius warming (31). "Rapid-intensification" resulted as Dorian's wind speeds increased over 35 mph in just twenty-four hours, and then it repeated this intensification (32). NASA has noted that the frequency and intensity of category 4 and 5 hurricanes have increased since the early 1980s.

Safe Home conducted a study that concluded that Florida and South Carolina are the two states most at risk for increasing climate impacts. Both states have long coastlines, making them more vulnerable to property damage and loss of life as global warming leads more frequent tropical storms and more severe hurricanes. The study noted inland portions of South Carolina are also at greater risk for more wildfires due to worsening drought conditions.

Florida has appropriated $200 million to find climate crisis solutions for sea-level rise and flood prevention, as sea levels are expected to rise by six feet by 2100. Miami already experiences severe "blue-sky" street flooding regularly (33).

More than 110 million people live below high-tide sea levels worldwide. By 2100, scientist predict there will be about 190 million people living below high-tide levels, exposing hundreds of millions of people to severe flooding. The worst climate consequences are projected to occur in Antarctica, China, Bangladesh, and India.

Many states, including Alaska, Texas, Arkansas, North and South Carolina, and Hawaii recently set new rainfall records. Alaska's newest record rainfall of 16.17 inches surpassed its previous high in 1989 by 2.26 inches. Texas received 60.58 inches of rain from Hurricane Harvey in 2017. South Carolina's newest record was 23.63 inches. North Carolina saw a record 35.93 inches. In 2018, Hawaii set a new rainfall record of 52.02 inches (34).

US Military Bases Are Being Severely Impacted by Climate Change

Michael T. Kare's new book, entitled *All Hell Breaking Loose: The Pentagon's Perspective on Climate Change* (Metropolitan Books, 2019), offers a wide-ranging review of the impact of the climate crisis on US military readiness. Climate change affects our interconnected world in the form of more storms, floods, extreme heat, and drought. Whole regions of the world will suffer food shortages, energy crises, pandemics, and mass migrations set off by global shock waves, which will wash away the ground from under fragile states and unravel international trade. The Pentagon has documented infrastructure vulnerabilities at seventy-nine key military facilities due to these increasing threats. Weakening infrastructure is a national security concern, as military bases will lose their rapid response capabilities to potential security threats. In 2007, the Pentagon's think tank study concluded that climate change is a "threat multiplier which increases the likelihood of internal unrest and state collapse" (35). It also could disrupt military training and operations due to increasingly extreme weather events, which contribute to instability in fragile regions of the world, increasing the need for humanitarian assistance missions.

On February 23, 2020, Carol Polsgrove noted for the Sierra Club that "as temperatures rise, melting ice [in the Arctic] opens up a repository of oil, gas and minerals. Two...nations bordering the Arctic are among the most powerful on Earth: the United States and Russia. China has an interest in potential Arctic sea lanes for trade with Europe. Other nations would like a share of the economic wealth created as a new ocean appears" (36). Polsgrove observed that the possibility of conflict in the Arctic is on the minds of military planners; in a recent article in the February 2020 *Military Review*, the authors argued for governance of the Arctic as a "global common" which would favor "environmental sustainability and climate change prevention" (36).

Polsgrove explained the irony here: "The US military itself is a major contributor to climate change." A 2019 US Army War College article admitted frankly that "the army is not an environmentally friendly organization." Given public concern about the environment, they argue that the Department of Defense should create "a culture of environmental stewardship across the force" (36).

The Environmental Consequences Are Staggering

Offshore fishing is being adversely impacted as ocean temperatures continue to rise. Fishing is a way of life for many coastal communities and a food source for hundreds of thousands. Commercial and recreational fishing contribute billions to national economies. Yet global fish stocks have shrunk by 4.1 percent in the past several years (37). Many species of fish are at risk due to rising water temperatures. More shrimp are developing "black gills" and becoming infected with parasites due to reduced oxygen levels in warmer waters (38).

GREAT SAND DUNES NATIONAL PARK, COLORADO

Tourism is being adversely affected by global warming. Montana's Glacier National Park was the home to 150 glaciers when the park was established. By 2015, the number of glaciers had declined to 26, according to the US Geological Survey (39). As the climate warms, more glaciers are disappearing. A new report shows that exotic travel produces much more carbon. Researchers at the Future Laboratory found that mass-marketing tourism will better address the climate crisis than exclusive resorts for the few who can afford it. By 2030, artificial islands that can produce their own food and water will offer no environmental impact as compared to exotic travel destinations (40). Many hotels like the Hilton Honors program are already offering "Go Green" plans, which award hotel guests bonus points if they agree to reduced room service.

The Florida Everglades faces a multipronged threat from drought, excessive air temperatures, and elevated salinity from sea-level rise, which kills the saw grass prairie, causing the underlying peat soil to collapse (41). Tourist attractions around the world are being adversely affected by severe storms, high winds, more frequent tornadoes, and coastal flooding. For many coastal communities, tourism provides jobs and tax revenues.

Rising Sea Levels Threaten Coastal Cities

Rising sea levels will soon make some of the world's most populous cities uninhabitable. Mumbai, Jakarta, Canton, Hong Kong, Shanghai, Lagos, Bangkok, and Manila are all at risk. In the United States, coastal cities including New Orleans, Louisiana; Miami, Florida; Charleston, South Carolina; and many others could force millions of residents to relocate to the interior of the country (42). Homes originally built in flood zones that suffer heavy damage will likely be condemned by local governments that bear much of the financial cost of cleanup.

Warming Oceans Threaten Our Health

Mirante do Leblon, Rio de Janeiro, Brazil

Warming oceans are also creating a breeding ground for deadly flesh-eating bacteria. Due to warming waters, deadly bacteria are flourishing in waters where they were never typically seen before. These bacteria, known as *V. vulnificus* and *A. Streptococcus* multiply in warm water that reaches temperatures higher than 55°F (43). These harmful bacteria typically enter the human body through a cut or open wound and quickly infect the surrounding soft tissue with the potential to develop into necrotizing fasciitis, which can be life threatening if not treated aggressively with antibiotics. The Delaware Bay hospital saw just one case of *V. vulnificus* infection from 2008 to 2016. During the summers of 2017 and 2018, there were five reported infections (44).

Half the world's sandy beaches could disappear by the end of the century due to climate change, according to researchers with the European Union's Joint Research Center (45). Global warming leads to higher ocean temperatures, which in turn lead to sea-level rise, resulting in more violent storms and hurricanes and causing greater beach erosion.

Toxic Algae Threatens Our Health

FOLLY BEACH, SOUTH CAROLINA

In Florida and Mississippi, many beaches are being invaded by harmful blue-green algal blooms called HABs, leading to beach closures (46). HABs comprise toxic algae that can trigger symptoms like nausea, cramping, vomiting, and skin rashes. Humans should avoid eating seafood that has been exposed to toxic algae. The National Oceanic and Atmospheric Administration reported an increase in toxic algae due to climate change and increasing nutrient pollution from fertilizer runoff.

Greenland's Ice Glaciers Are Melting

On February 20, 2019, the temperature in Greenland climbed above freezing and stayed there for over twenty-four hours (47). Greenland's ice glaciers are melting into the surrounding oceans. The polar bear population is threatened by the destruction of their habitat and will likely face extinction due to melting ice caused by higher temperatures. Melting Arctic ice is also releasing various toxic pollutants, including mercury, into the marine environment. NASA predicts that by 2050, there will be no more sea ice floating in the Arctic Ocean during the summer months.

Scientists have discovered cracks in Greenland's ice sheets that have been melting. Drones have shown that water is flowing through the cracks in the ice sheets, creating waterfalls. Researchers from the United Kingdom have filmed footage of meltwater lakes on the ice sheets, draining five million cubic meters of water from the ice sheet surface in just five hours. That is enough water to fill two thousand Olympic-size pools (48). The Greenland ice melting is occurring six times faster than melting that occurred in 1980.

Arctic Ice Is Also Melting

Cruise ships and charter boats are now sailing across melting Arctic waters, creating dangerous situations for passengers. A cruise ship called the *Clipper Adventurer* ran aground on a large rock formation that was not shown on existing maps (49). The number of cargo ships traversing Canadian Arctic waters nearly doubled in the last decade, thanks to hotter summers that now melt even so-called "multiyear" ice, which used to stay frozen year round.

Glaciers Are Melting

Anthropologists discovered that the Okjökull Glacier in Iceland has melted due to human-caused climate change. This little glacier on a little mountain, in a country far away on the edge of the world, indicates a much larger story that affects the entire planet. A memorial has been dedicated to the

Okjökull Glacier as a reminder to the human population of the consequences of global warming (50).

The Pizol Glacier in Switzerland's Glarus Alps has also lost its status as a glacier but has left behind 26,000 square meters of ice. The Pizol Glacier measured 2,700 meters in length before it lost 90 percent of its size due to melting (51). The Swiss Association for Climate Protection obtained 120,000 signatures—above the 100,000 required—needed to launch a popular initiative demanding that Switzerland reduce its greenhouse gas emissions to zero by 2050 (52).

The Thwaites Glacier in West Antarctica is also melting at very rapid pace due to warm seawater underneath the ice. Scientists drilled into the glacier and measured the water temperature underneath at 32°F/0°C (53). The Thwaites Glacier, once larger than the state of Pennsylvania, now poses a threat to passing vessels as the glacier breaks up into smaller floating pieces of ice.

DIXIE PLANTATION, HOLLYWOOD, SOUTH CAROLINA

Global Warming Is Taking Its Toll on Infrastructure, Agriculture, and Forests

When California weather turns excessively hot and strong winds increase, so does the chance of wildfires. In October of 2019, PG&E turned their electric customers' power off in thirty-four counties to prevent sparking new wildfires because the massive utility had been blamed for previous wildfires that led to multiple deaths and massive destruction. These temporary power outages inconvenienced hundreds of businesses. Public schools had to close.

Scientists predict that by 2040, one in four steel bridges in the United States could collapse as a result of extreme heat, which causes expansion joints to pull apart and become clogged with dirt and debris, creating a serious public safety hazard (54).

Wildfires Are More Intense and More Frequent

California wildfires have become much larger and more intense in recent years. Large cities like Los Angeles, Sonoma, and Calabasas are being affected by these destructive fires. Five out of California's twenty deadliest wildfires have occurred during the last two years.

Ten of the twenty most destructive wildfires on record have occurred during the past decade (55). Thousands of families have been forced to evacuate their homes, leaving behind all their personal belongings. The number of fallen victims from the wildfires is continuing to rise as the fires are continuously breaking out and spreading. For several years, California has been extremely dry and humid due to a lack of rainfall, coupled with unusually high winds and rising temperatures. These conditions have resulted in wildfires that spread rapidly with increasing frequency and severity. Francesca Dominici, codirector of the Harvard Data Science Initiative, predicts that absent aggressive mitigation measures taken to slow the release of greenhouse gas emissions, smoke from wildfires will also increase in intensity (56).

Australian bushfires, which raged for weeks in late 2019, burned over 12.5 million acres, destroying hundreds of homes and killing forty people. The intensity and duration of these Australian bushfires has also been linked to global warming, which led to reduced rainfall amounts and caused widespread drought, according to Mike Flannigan, a scientist with the University of Alberta (57).

Toxic Waste Sites Are Being Impacted

The US Governmental Accounting Office (GAO), a nonpartisan congressional watchdog, has identified over one thousand toxic waste sites that could be impacted by large forest fires and widespread flooding. The GAO has recommended to Congress that the Environmental Protection Agency (EPA) should accept more responsibility and accountability in cleaning up these waste sites (58). Mathy Stanislaus, who formerly worked with the EPA, has recommended installing protective rubber caps to cover these toxic waste dumps to keep water from infiltrating the waste, causing it to spread into the ground water (59).

Different Regions of the United States Are Experiencing Different Impacts

NASA has reported how different regions of the United States will be affected by global warming.

- **The Southeast** will experience sea-level rise, which will pose threats to the local economy and environment. Tornadoes in the Southeast are getting worse. Unlike the Plains, where an approaching tornado can be seen coming, the Southeast has more trees, which can make it more difficult to see a tornado approaching. Tornadoes in this area stay on the ground for longer periods and move faster when they are being pushed by the jet stream. CNN meteorologists have said this puts more pressure on them to forecast timely tornado warnings. Many homes in the Southeast have no basements available to take cover. There are also many mobile homes and manufactured homes in the Southeast, making their occupants more vulnerable to wind speeds in excess of 50 mph (80 kph).

Moab, Utah

Agriculture is being adversely affected by warmer winters. In 2016, Georgia peach farmers lost 80 percent of their crop because it was too warm to grow peaches. Blueberries also were hurt by the warmer weather. Farmers are now researching hybrids that can grow with fewer low chill hours, according to Pam Knox, an agricultural climatologist at the University of Georgia. Beekeepers are experiencing issues with the warmer winters, too, as bees are expending more energy by eating more of their own stored honey. The mosquito population grows larger since there is not enough cold weather to kill off large parts of the population, which causes the spread of diseases like Zika and dengue. Declining water supplies, reduced agricultural production, and health impacts will be the norm due to increased heat, flooding, and erosion along coastal areas (60).

- **The Southwest** can expect to see increased heat, drought, and insect outbreaks. Agriculture continues to be impacted by decreased water supplies because the snowpack is melting earlier, preventing reservoirs from storing more of the spring runoff. The Colorado River's average annual flow has already declined by 20 percent as mountain snowpacks disappear due to warmer temperatures, according to Juliet Eilperin with the *Washington Post* (61).

FISHERMAN'S TRAIL, VICENTINA, PORTUGAL

The Colorado River's decline impacts about forty million residents in the American West who depend on the river to supply drinking water for Colorado's largest cities.

- **The Northwest** is expected to experience a reduction in water supplies and streamflow. Sea-level rise and erosion will increase the risk to infrastructure. Increasing ocean acidity pose major threats to fishing and wildlife. Increasing wildfire, insect outbreaks, and tree diseases will cause increasing tree die-off (60).

- **The Midwest** region will experience higher temperatures, heavy precipitation and damaged soil. Freezing has historically stopped microbes from breaking down organic matter in the soil. Michigan's cherry trees are struggling as a result of the warmer winters (60).

- **The Mountain West** has suffered massive tree loss due to an increase in bark beetles, which attack pine and spruce trees. Historically, the cold winter kills of the bark beetles. Warmer weather coupled with low precipitation make trees more vulnerable to the bark beetle. The ski industry is also seeing shortened ski seasons as the fall season lasts longer, and spring comes earlier.

- **The Northeast** will experience more heat waves, heavy precipitation, and rising sea levels. Infrastructure, agriculture, fisheries, and ecosystems will be increasingly compromised. In Maine, ice fishing, skiing, and snowmobiling seasons are being cut short due to warming temperatures. The tick population increases with global warming, which affects not only wildlife but human outdoor activities since deer ticks can transmit Lyme disease (60).

Chapter 3

IMPACTS ON WILDLIFE

The Endangered Species List Is Growing Longer Each Year

GHOST CRAB, FOLLY BEACH, SOUTH CAROLINA

According to the International Union of Conservation for Nature (IUCN), several different species are at risk for extinction. It has estimated that one out of every four species are at risk of becoming extinct. The ICUN assessed several different groups of species and examined the likelihood of extinction. The results revealed that amphibians have a 40 percent chance of becoming extinct due to climate change (62). Amphibians are cold-blooded animals that depend on heat from the sun. They enjoy living in wet, moist conditions such as rain forests and wetlands. With rising temperatures drying out their habitats, they do not have a high chance of survival. Sharks and stingrays have a 31 percent chance of becoming extinct. Seawater is becoming warmer and therefore contains fewer nutrients. Crustaceans, lobsters, freshwater crabs, freshwater crayfishes, and freshwater shrimps all have a 27 percent chance of becoming extinct due to warming temperatures and an overall changing climate (63).

Whales and Sea Lions Are at Risk of Extinction

Recently, more than a hundred gray whales washed up dead on West Coast beaches. Scientists say that the West Coast has seen an unusually high number of deaths in marine animals. The Marine Mammal Center reported it rescued 370 California sea lions during 2019 (64). When the sea lions wash up to the shore, it is obvious that they have been suffering from malnutrition, as there are fewer nutrients in the warmer water.

The salmon population is also in decline in the Sea of Okhotsk off the Shiretoko Peninsula in Japan, as the volume of sea ice is declining due to global warming. This area has some of the densest water on Earth because the sea ice leaves huge amounts of salt in the frigid waters. It travels east, carrying oxygen, iron, and other key nutrients to marine life in the northern Pacific Ocean. Near the island of Hokkaido, the salmon population has declined from approximately sixty-eight million in 2003 down to around twenty-eight million by 2018 (65). Salmon, which were historically found in the Sea of Okhotsk, have migrated to cooler seawater temperatures.

Birds Are at Risk Due to Climate Change

PLAYA ESCONDIDA, PANAMA

Two-thirds of the bird population could become extinct if the temperature warms by 3°C, according to a National Audubon Society study. Eagles, orioles, grouse, and gulls are all being adversely affected by global warming. The United States and Canada combined have lost around three million birds in the last fifty years due to dwindling food sources, severe wildfires, and intense hurricanes, which have displaced millions of birds due to habitat destruction (66).

Butterflies Are Dwindling in Number

The butterfly population is also at risk due to drastic climate changes across the United States, Canada, and Mexico. The lifecycle of a butterfly is driven by a search for optimal weather conditions, with temperatures between 50° to 70°F (67). Butterflies spend their summers in the United States and in Canada but then migrate to Central Mexico in the winter. Central Mexico is experiencing more winter storms due to warmer air over the Pacific Ocean. In 2002, about 75 percent of the monarch butterfly population died due to the severe winter weather (67). Monarch observers are seeing fewer butterflies migrating south in the winter due to Mexico's changing weather patterns.

Chapter 4

IMPACTS ON HUMANS

Mental Health Issues Are Increasing Due to Global Warming
Suicide rates, chronic anxiety, and severe depression have all increased as the Earth's temperature has risen. Some people are experiencing "solastalgia," which is defined as distress resulting from environmental changes (68). Psychologists believe that extremely high temperatures are detrimental to mental health. In 2014, Canadian researchers found that emergency room visits for mental issues increased by 29 percent during periods of extreme heat in Toronto. In 2016, Vietnamese scientists found that risk of admission to a mental health facility increased by 36 percent during weeklong heat waves (69). More young children are reportedly becoming anxious and afraid about the lasting effects of living in a world impacted by climate change. Mental health professionals have labeled this fear *eco-anxiety.*

Respiratory Health Is in Decline Due to Increasing Air Pollutants Worldwide
Lung disease and asthma conditions are exacerbated by increasing particulate matter in our polluted air due to greenhouse gas emissions. Heart and brain health will also be impacted as temperatures continue to rise. With increasingly polluted air, many people in India and China are already struggling to breathe without masks. Wildfires dramatically increase the number of microscopic particles and are especially dangerous to children and the elderly who suffer from preexisting heart or respiratory conditions.

Seattle has recently opened clean air centers as a result of the increased smoke from wildfires (70). Higher temperatures have increased the prevalence of mosquito-borne illnesses, including malaria and yellow dengue, fever which can be potentially deadly.

Heatstroke and Heart Attacks Are Becoming More Prevalent Due to Excessive Heat

Pennsylvania and California have seen higher mortality rates during times of extreme heat. British researchers found mortality rates from heart attack, stroke, and pneumonia increased steadily with temperatures over 70°F. Proteins in the human body begin to break down when temperatures exceed 104°F, which can lead to heatstroke (71). Scientists predict that by 2050, most days in many parts of the world will feel like 104°F. Dehydration is also a risk with extreme temperatures and heat waves. Dehydration can be deadly in severe cases.

Lyme Disease is Spreading Due to Climate Change

Climate change is contributing to an increase in Lyme disease outbreaks due to an increase in tick populations. A person can get infected with Lyme disease once they have been bitten by an infected tick. The Centers for Disease Control and Prevention (CDC) has warned that medical costs from treating Lyme disease infections may reach several billion dollars annually (72).

Psychiatric patients are more likely to die during heat waves. The scientific definition for a "heat wave," which could cause heatstroke, is defined as a period of three or more days with a maximum temperature of 89°F or more (73). Psychiatric patients will obviously need to have access to air-conditioning and close monitoring of medication use. Even without antipsychotics, scientists believe that psychiatric disorders alone can lead to death during a heat wave. Patients with chronic depression or schizophrenia are more likely to experience mental agitation that comes with intense heat waves (73).

Outdoor Activities Are Being Curtailed by Extreme Heat

When outdoor temperatures exceed 100°F, more people are forced to remain indoors. Sunlight in moderation produces more Vitamin D in our bodies, which is essential for the absorption of calcium, according to Dr. Clifford Rosen, MD, an osteoporosis researcher at the Maine Medical Center Research Institute. A Swedish study in the *Journal of Internal Medicine* monitored thirty thousand women over twenty years and found that those who spent more time outside lived six months to two years longer than those who had less sun exposure. With excessive heat, the Earth's population will likely get less and less sun exposure (74).

Children Are Raising Awareness with Their Protests

Children around the world have been protesting to raise public awareness about climate change. On September 20, 2019, many children skipped school at John Marshall Park in Washington, DC. School officials warned students that attending climate change protests would be considered as "unexcused" absences. CNN reported that several students said they were willing to accept the consequences to participate in these climate change protests as they held signs that read "There Is No Planet B" and "What Would Your Kids Say?" (75).

Concentration and Focus Are Being Affected by Extreme Heat

Rising temperatures are causing children to lose focus in the classroom. Teachers in areas experiencing record heat waves have noted diminishing student attention spans. A national survey of American students found that hotter school days also result in lower standardized test scores. One teacher in Denver, Colorado, observed that her students were "very sleepy and were having to get up to drink water quite often" during a recent heat wave (76). Children will understandably struggle in their studies when they are fatigued from extreme temperatures. Researchers examined whether standardized test performance on the SAT and PSAT had been affected by extreme heat. After looking at twenty-one million standardized test scores over fourteen years, test results that correlating with record high temperatures on the day the tests were administered confirmed that extreme heat resulted in lower test scores. Colder days did not adversely impact student test performance. Test scores were the highest when the temperature ranged between 60° to 70°F (76)

When a student experiences at least six school days with temperatures above 90°F, there's a corresponding reduction in academic performance. During 2019, many schools were forced to cancel classes because of the extremely high temperatures. Teachers from Madison, Wisconsin, to Oakland, California, even resorted to cutting off classroom lights to cope with these high temperatures. Kentucky schools suspended most outdoor activities during the extreme heat wave, fearing the potential threat to student health (76).

TELLURIDE, COLORADO

In September of 2019, the average temperature across the lower forty-eight states was 68.5°F, which is 3.5° above the twentieth century average. New Mexico, Texas, Ohio, Colorado, and Louisiana broke long-standing records for the highest September temperatures ever recorded. Atlanta, Georgia, saw temperatures rise 12° above average for the month of September. Thirty-seven states experienced above-average temperatures during the month of September in 2019 (77).

Violent Crime Rates Are Expected to Increase with Rising Temperatures

Criminologists have documented that violent crime rates increase in the hot summer months by 5.7 percent on days with maximum daily temperatures above 85°F (29.4°C) compared to days below that threshold (78).

Drought and Starvation Have Become Much Worse Due to Climate Change

In Guatemala, the rainy season normally lasts from April to October, with an only an occasional dry spell during the summer months. But the past ten years have brought more droughts with higher temperatures, which has made life difficult for farmers. In 2018, drought-related crop failures in Guatemala caused extreme food shortages for some 840,000 people (79).

Air Pollution Continues to Cause Adverse Health Consequences

Thirty years ago, fossil fuels made up 81 percent of the world's energy portfolio. Despite hundreds of billions of dollars spent on renewable energy, fossil fuels still make up 81 percent of the world's energy production. Air pollution resulting from these fossil fuel emissions continues to result in negative consequences for human health. The EPA defines "particulate matter" as the mix of solid and liquid droplets floating in the air. As fossil fuels burn from forest fires, from automobiles, from power plants and construction sites, particulate matter is released into the air. When the human body inhales these invisible particles, they become trapped in our lungs, causing difficulty breathing and shortness of breath. Inhaled carcinogens can even lead to lung cancer. The amount of particulate matter can vary depending upon the geographic location and the time of year. Air pollution results in a higher death rate than either traffic accidents or homicides (80).

Chapter 5

HOW CLIMATE CHANGE EFFECTS THE REST OF THE WORLD

Methane Is a Harmful Greenhouse Gas and a Large Contributor to Global Warming

According to *Science Daily*, methane emissions have increased by 150 percent over the past three hundred years. These emissions originate from natural sources as well as from human activity. Methane has a relatively short life of about nine years, while carbon dioxide stays in the atmosphere for almost a century. Fossil methane can remain sequestered for millions of years in carbon deposits in the permafrost. Biological methane is released naturally from wetlands or from landfills, livestock, and rice fields. Scientists measure the amount of methane being emitted into our atmosphere, but tracking the source of the methane can sometimes be difficult. Researchers know that fossil fuel methane is one of the largest components. If researchers can find a way to capture methane emissions from fossil fuel extraction, it could have a substantial impact on lowering future global warming (81).

The provisions of the Clean Air Act of 1963 lowered air pollution levels by mandating reductions in the level of pollutants like nitrogen dioxide, sulfur dioxide, and carbon monoxide (81). Prior to the Clean Air Act, many states did not meet the air quality standards. Unfortunately, the Trump administration has lessened EPA enforcement of many of the regulations that resulted from passage of the Clean Air Act.

Financial Impacts around the World Could Be Staggering

Climate change is becoming problematic for states and local governments to borrow money for infrastructure projects like roads, bridges, dams, levies, and seawalls. Moody's Corporation is one of the largest US ratings agencies. It has recently adopted a policy of including the effects of climate change into its credit risk assessments. In 2018, the United States saw more than $91 billion in property damages from the costliest storms, droughts, hurricanes, floods, and wildfires on record, according to the National Oceanic and Atmospheric Administration.

Investors and insurance companies are now relying on Moody's ratings to factor in the financial risks associated with the impact of climate change in a geographic market. Federal flood insurance premiums will also have to take into consideration the impact of rising sea levels and increasing storms, particularly in flood-prone areas (82).

Developing Nations Are Being Negatively Impacted by Climate Change

The Warsaw International Mechanism was established in 2013 to financially compensate developing nations for the harm being caused by the developed nations from climate change. The structure of this agreement provided a mechanism for "developed countries to provide developing countries with finance, technology and capacity-building to help victims of climate change recover after extreme weather events or slower-onset climate disasters such as sea-level rise. As the number and strength of natural disasters increased, several developed nations no longer want to be on the hook for the financial losses of the weaker, developing nations. The developed nations have advocated for some type of insurance mechanism to compensate the developing countries who are suffering extreme financial losses due to climate change" (83).

Developing nations are expected to be the most impacted by climate change because they do not possess the resources to become resilient or recover from natural disasters. Developing nations include small islands in the Caribbean and the South Pacific, and in countries in Asia, Africa, and Latin America. These developing nations are dependent on their natural resources to meet their everyday needs for shelter, food and clothing. Natural disasters have a disproportionately negative impact on these developing nations. Many homes destroyed in developing nations will never be rebuilt without financial assistance or loan guarantees from the developed nations.

Clean Portable Water Shortages Are Occurring because of the Climate Crisis

There are already more than 1.7 billion people without access to clean water. With a warming climate and the natural disasters that are expected to follow, the number of people without access to clean water is expected to reach five billion. The subtropics will most likely be hit the hardest with droughts, evaporation, unpredictable rainfall, and runoff (84).

The international financial system could face serious risks if climate change accelerates. Natural disasters like hurricanes, massive flooding, wildfires, and tropical storms can cause billions in property damage. These future risks must be factored into investment decisions. Scientists have predicted that if the Earth warms by 4°C, the economic losses could exceed $23 trillion per year. These predictions can be compared to the 2007–2008 financial crisis and would be far worse. Financial institutions could play a large role in mitigating climate change, but so far, only a few have made financial commitments (85).

Banks Are Beginning to See the Light

Larry Fink with the global investment management company BlackRock has seen a shift in corporate policy considerations. Goldman Sachs was the first bank to announce that they will stop offering loans to new coal-fired power plants. Nor will the bank provide money or advice to firms making most of their revenue from coal projects (86). Wells Fargo and JPMorgan Chase have both adopted similar position statements taking those banks out of funding oil and gas drilling in the Arctic region. Banks have become targets for environmental activists who have attacked their business practices of providing billions to finance fossil fuel projects around the world. Many large corporations are investing in clean energy projects while scaling back on fossil fuel involvement to appease climate-conscious investors. Businesses around the world are reassessing and adjusting their mission statements to account for the adverse effects of climate change (87).

Climate Change Adversely Impacts Outdoor Sporting Events

During the 2020 Australian Open, extremely high temperatures and smoke from the massive bushfires affected professional tennis players' ability to perform outdoors. These unhealthy conditions resulted in officials moving some of the matches indoors (88). Olympic officials are now concerned about how extreme heat will affect the 2020 Summer Olympics. The International Olympic Committee has recognized that climate change is a concern for host city selection for future games. Less than half of the previous Olympic host cities are expected to be cold enough to host the Olympic Winter Games (89).

Florida Citrus Industry Is Being Adversely Impacted by Climate Change

Citrus groves in Florida are at risk from a bacterium known as huanglongbing. This bacterium is most likely caused by warming temperatures, which leads to "citrus greening" and prevents the citrus fruit from ripening. Many citrus farmers are abandoning their farms due to this bacterial outbreak causing citrus greening. Researchers are working on the problem by frantically trying to develop new root stocks so that trees can better tolerate disease. They hope to genetically engineer new types of oranges to replace traditional varieties that are more vulnerable to citrus greening. Tropicana Orange Juice and Minute Maid Orange Juice have experienced over $5 billion in losses as citrus production has declined. Their parent companies, Coca-Cola and PepsiCo, may be forced to buy oranges from Brazil or Costa Rica if the bacterium continues to spread in Florida (90).

South Carolina Agriculture Is Being Hurt by the Climate Crisis

Agriculture is South Carolina's leading industry. The state has more than twenty-five thousand farms spread out over 4.9 million acres. During the past decade, the state has experienced more summer heat days exceeding 100°F. This excessive heat has severely impacted crop production. During South Carolina's 2019 growing season, tomatoes, watermelons, squash, soybeans, and corn were all severely damaged by excessive temperatures, resulting in substantial financial losses that were not always covered by crop insurance (91).

Insurance Industry Is Being Impacted by Climate Change

Insurance companies are withdrawing from those areas considered to be at risk to climate change. Areas prone to wildfire, flooding, and severe storms are being reclassified as high-risk areas. Allstate Insurance and State Farm Insurance have both decided not to renew certain insurance policies in these areas, affecting more than four hundred thousand customers. Many of these policies were written in California, where severe wildfires have caused billions in property losses. Coastal areas that are being battered by intense hurricanes and tropical storms are also experiencing insurance cancellations as homeowner policies come up for renewal (93).

Extreme Heat Waves Are Expected to Worsen

In the summer months of 2019, India experienced a deadly heat wave that killed over one hundred people when temperatures exceeded 120°. Other countries are experiencing record high temperatures as the deadly effects of global warming accelerate (94).

Larger cities with populations are at greater risk for more extreme temperature days due to the urban heating effect, in which concrete and asphalt radiate heat. By the middle of the twenty-first century, climatologists are predicting there will be ninety-seven days on average when temperatures climb above 100°F. Each year, larger cities will experience seventy-one days on average when temperatures rise above 105°F (95).

If global temperatures rise 3°C by 2050, 55 percent of the world's population across 35 percent of its land area are expected to experience more than twenty days of lethal heat per year. West Africa and parts of the Middle East are expected to experience some of the highest temperatures because they are closer to the equator. It is estimated that there could be one hundred days of deadly heat throughout the year, potentially killing millions (96).

Nigeria, Haiti, Manila, Kiribati, Yemen, and the United Arab Emirates are expected to experience some of the worst consequences of climate change. During the summer months in Yemen, temperatures typically reach above 110°F (97).

Haiti is at great risk for worsening hurricanes, landslides, contaminated fresh water, and a decrease in agricultural productivity. Steep mountains across the region make Haiti susceptible to landslides. Many citizens in Haiti are dependent on locally grown agriculture. However, with an increase in hurricanes and natural disasters, agriculture is at risk. Climate change has adversely impacted the Haitian economy, which is still recovering from previous natural disasters (97).

Manila in the Philippines is another region projected to be significantly impacted by climate change. Earthquakes and hurricanes continue to impact Manila's infrastructure. Manila is prone to extreme flooding in times of heavy rain and hurricanes, which is made worse due to its ineffective drainage systems. Illness and disease are likely to spread due to flooding and the lack of sanitation in the area. These adverse conditions will significantly impact Manila, causing many of its citizens to be displaced by 2050 (97).

The 2100 Project: An Atlas for A Green New Deal predicts that the largest losses will occur in regions that are already in poverty. Mississippi, Arkansas, Texas, and several coastal states will be more adversely affected by climate change. Arkansas will be affected the most due to the impact of drought, heat, soil erosion, and heavy rain, which all damage agriculture. In Mississippi, there are countless bodies of water that put the state at risk for coastal flooding. Mississippi's agriculture will also be destroyed by the flooding that they will most likely occur. Mississippi citizens may even have to migrate due to the potential effects of climate change. Additionally, up to one hundred million non-US citizens could have to migrate to the United States because their homes could be compromised by climate change (98).

Sea Cliff Collapses Are Occurring More Often Due to Climate Change

Several California sea cliffs collapsing during the late summer months of 2019. Tragically, three people were killed near Encinitas, California, when a sea cliff collapsed. California is falling piece by piece into the Pacific with the worsening climate crisis. Scientists believe that nearly three-quarters of California's coastlines are actively eroding, putting lives, homes, roadways, railways, utilities, and other infrastructure in danger. Rising sea levels are to blame for falling cliffs, which are a direct consequence of global warming (99).

Melting Permafrost Is Releasing More Carbon Dioxide

Permafrost is frozen soil located in the Northern Hemisphere, and it absorbs large amounts of carbon dioxide that would otherwise be trapped in the atmosphere. With rising temperatures, permafrost is melting. Researchers predict that two-thirds of the Earth's permafrost likely will disappear by 2200 as a result of global warming. This has the potential to unleash vast quantities of carbon dioxide and methane into the atmosphere. Permafrost stores twice as much carbon dioxide than what exists in the atmosphere, so a meltdown would release roughly 190 billion tons of carbon in the next one hundred years. Studies also confirm the amount expected to be released by permafrost melting is equivalent to half the amount of carbon released since the dawn of the Industrial Age (100).

Extreme Summer Heat in Texas Caused Electric Power Disruptions

During the summer of 2019, the Electric Reliability Council of Texas encouraged its utility customers to decrease energy use during the hottest periods of the day. *The Texas Observer* reported during this period that Texas used more megawatts of energy in the summer of 2019 than a decade earlier, causing dramatic increases in energy consumption (101).

Section Two:
The Global Solutions

Chapter 6

REDUCING EMISSIONS AND BECOMING ENERGY EFFICIENT

Better Energy Efficiency in Homes, Businesses and Commercial Buildings

Energy efficiency can help address climate change. The UN estimates that by 2025, there will be 8.5 billion people on Earth (102). A growing world population brings drastic increases in fossil fuel consumption—which means more gasoline-powered vehicles, more food consumed, more homes constructed, more clean water needed, more electricity produced, more everything. Practicing energy efficiency will be crucial to reducing energy consumption and CO_2 emissions. Without increased energy efficiency investments, energy consumption and related emissions will be 60 percent higher, resulting in consumers paying $800 billion more per year in energy costs (102).

Building codes should require that new home construction include more insulation and energy-efficient glass windows. Home builders could be incentivized by tax credits if they install energy-efficient appliances, insulated glass, and increased insulation materials. Unfortunately, many lower-income families see these up-front costs as a barrier and refuse to participate in implementing energy-efficient appliances. About 15 percent of Americans currently live in poverty (103). For families living in poverty, it will be financially difficult for them to replace outdated air-conditioning units and inefficient water heaters. Investor-owned utilities need to improve energy-efficiency programs that provide financial assistance to those living in poverty.

Low-income households spend $1.23 per square foot on their utility bills, while all other households spend $0.98 per square foot. With outdated appliances, the prices and amount of energy used will always be higher. Besides income, there are other factors that affect low-income-earning families' ability to practice energy efficiency. Two of these factors include language barriers and health and safety issues. Mold and floodwater damage can limit resources for poorer households to install energy-efficient appliances (104).

In Portland, Oregon, a nonprofit organization called Verde Landscape is assisting those with low incomes and language barriers by providing jobs for those who have no job skills. They are offered work on landscaping projects, building bioswales and rain gardens using native plants to absorb and filter rainfall to mitigate stormwater flooding (105).

Households can practice energy efficiency by installing light-emitting diode (LED) bulbs. Incandescent light bulbs transmit light for about twelve hundred hours. An LED bulb can transmit light for around twenty-five thousand hours. Incandescent lights use 60 watts of electricity. LED bulbs use only 10 watts. Incandescent bulbs are replaced about four times per year. LED light bulbs can last up to five years (106). According to a study conducted by Project Drawdown, using LED bulbs is equivalent to taking 75.7 million vehicles off the road (107).

The *Energy-Efficient Home Design Trends 2019 Report* noted that homeowners are motivated to save money on their utility bills by purchasing tankless water heaters, energy-efficient refrigerators, dishwashers, and washers and dryers, which can all substantially reduce energy usage (108).

Geoengineering May Buy the Earth a "Cooling-Off" Period

Researchers are considering geoengineering for ways to cool the planet. One method would involve spraying shiny droplets or reflective particles into the atmosphere to deflect the sun's heat from reaching the Earth's surface. It is estimated this process could cost up to one hundred billion dollars. Scientists concede that this will not provide a permanent solution for global warming, but it could buy us some time to find more permanent climate solutions (109).

Offshore Wind Turbines Are Providing Substantially More Renewable Energy

In China, General Electric is building a 715-megawatt offshore wind farm capable of powering over five hundred thousand homes (110). Staten Island, New York City, is seeking funding for an offshore wind port facility. Atlantic Offshore Terminals plans to purchase a thirty-acre property for this new port facility. New York could eventually become the hub of for the multibillion-dollar offshore wind industry. The market for offshore wind is expected to exceed $70 billion in spending over the next twenty years. New York and New Jersey will likely comprise 60 percent of that market (111).

SAN JOSÉ PROVINCE, COSTA RICA

Carbon Neutral Communities Are Leading the Way

Copenhagen plans to become one of the first carbon-neutral cities by the year 2025. Many families are changing their lifestyles to reduce their carbon footprint. Some examples include families raising chickens in the backyard for their eggs, brewing coffee using electricity generated from wind turbines, and commuting to work or school by riding bikes. Copenhagen has installed extensive bike lanes, making cycling easier and safer (112).

Utah's Roadmap

MOAB, UTAH

The state of Utah has adopted a plan called the Utah Roadmap, intended to reduce greenhouse gas emissions by 25 percent below 2005 levels by the year 2025. Utah hopes to eventually reduce emissions by 80 percent by 2050 by phasing out coal burning plants and by encouraging drivers to switch to electric vehicles (113).

CDP'S Climate Action Scores Can Raise Awareness

CDP, a nonprofit organization that is working to reduce carbon emissions worldwide, assigned "climate action scores" to over eight thousand businesses. Businesses receiving top climate action scores included Microsoft, Citigroup, Walmart, and Alphabet. European businesses had the highest number of perfect scores. The United States had thirty-five businesses receiving a perfect score. Japan had thirty-eight businesses that were awarded a perfect score. CDP hopes to raise awareness and build a sense of competitiveness among nations to become more energy efficient.

Minneapolis Is Promoting Energy Efficiency for New Home Buyers

In Minneapolis, Minnesota, homebuyers will have the opportunity to see how energy efficient each house is before they purchase it. The higher the score, the more resilient the house will be to weather extremes. Homes with high energy scores could save homeowners more than 30 percent on their energy bills. The Minneapolis Division of Sustainability is providing these energy reports as a public service to home buyers and to raise awareness about energy efficiency (114).

Virginia Adopts a "Clean Economy Act"

In 2019, the Virginia Legislature adopted the Virginia Clean Economy Act, which adopted several public policy initiatives to address climate change. Virginia has been adversely impacted by severe flooding disasters in recent years. The legislature's goal is to eliminate greenhouse gas emissions in Virginia by 2050. Part of the plan adopts the Regional Greenhouse Gas Initiative, which puts a tax on emitting carbon dioxide. Virginia has incentivized investor-owned utility companies to provide more resources for energy-efficiency programs and shift investments away from fossil fuels toward renewable sources like solar and wind power (115).

Many Large Corporations Are Implementing Energy-Efficiency Standards

In the United States, more major corporations are pledging to practice energy efficiency and reduce their carbon dioxide emissions. Starbucks has announced its plan to limit food waste and water usage while also cutting greenhouse gas emissions in half by the year of 2030 (116).

Microsoft has pledged to not only reduce emissions but become "carbon negative" by 2030 (117). Starbucks's decision is a result of internal environmental concerns coupled with activist pressure. Many other companies are following suit by implementing their own green goals to address climate change.

Many environmentally conscious consumers are rewarding companies that adopt corporate goals aligned with addressing global warming and climate change when making a purchase. More private businesses are now including carbon reduction plans into their corporate strategies. These businesses are hoping to see significant benefits, including increased innovation, competitiveness, risk management, and sales growth. Some restaurants are now offering their patrons an eco-friendly menu. Many grocery stores are using positive reinforcement for their eco-friendly shoppers by offering discounts to customers who bring their own reusable shopping bags in place of the store's plastic bags.

Colgate, one of the largest toothpaste companies, has designed a recyclable toothpaste bottle. (118). Colgate has released their recyclable toothpaste bottle under their brand of all-natural products called Tom's of Maine. By 2025, all of Colgate's toothpaste bottles will be recyclable across all brands (118). The company not only wants to implement this new technology within their own brand, but they want to share it with other companies once they know it will be a success.

Planting One Trillion Trees Worldwide Could Help Reverse Deforestation

PANAMA

Planting more trees is a successful strategy to mitigate the effects of climate change. When CO2 becomes stuck in the upper atmosphere, global warming intensifies. One tree can trap a ton of carbon dioxide during its lifetime. There are several types of trees with high rates of CO2 absorption. US examples include eucalyptus in Hawaii, loblolly pine in the Southeast, bottomland hardwoods in Mississippi, and poplars (aspens) in the Great Lakes region. Trees with a faster growth rate can absorb more CO2 (119). Bamboo is one of the fastest-growing plants in the world, and it is excellent at absorbing CO2. Bamboo grows best in tropical and subtropical climates (120).

In 2019, European researchers identified over 6.5 million square miles of open land where trees could be planted that are not currently being used for agriculture or urban development (121). If this were to happen, these new forests could sequester about two-thirds of all the carbon released by humans since the start of the Industrial Revolution, reducing carbon dioxide in the atmosphere by 25 percent (122). Because trees are slow growers, tree planting on open land would need to begin almost immediately to have this kind of significant impact on global warming.

Deforestation practices in Brazil and elsewhere are wiping out the Amazon rain forest. Deforestation accelerated more than 60 percent in just one year, between 2018 to 2019, as local farmers cut down or burned forests to plant crops or raise cattle (123).

Since the rubber boom in the nineteenth century, followed by the gold rush, expanding ranching, more damming and logging have all resulted in the loss of nearly 1,000,000 square kilometers of the Amazon. In May of 2019 alone, 769 square kilometers of the Amazon were lost (124). The Brazilian government has announced plans to construct massive dams, creating large lakes, which will result in more deforestation. The Belo Monte Dam in Brazil has already resulted in a 55 percent reduction in Brazilian rain forests (124). The consequences of deforestation include less rainfall and higher temperatures in Brazil, Uruguay, Paraguay, and Argentina, leading to extreme temperatures followed by extreme droughts.

In August of 2019, the Amazon rain forests burned for weeks on end. Many of these fires were intentionally set by loggers and ranchers to clear land for their cattle. Brazil produces and exports large amounts of meat to the rest of the world. In 2018, Brazil exported 1.64 million pounds of beef, which was the highest volume in history (125). Historically, the Amazon was moist and humid during the summer months of July and August. Due to climate change, the rain forest's conditions have changed, as the fires continue to spread rapidly all over the forests due to hot and dry conditions. The CO2 that has been stored in the Amazon trees for years has now been released back into the atmosphere. Forty-eight hours after the initial fire had started, there were twenty-five hundred active fires in the Brazilian rain forest (126). The smoke emitting from the forest was so vast that it could be seen from outer space. The flames released pollutants, particulate matter, and toxic gases, including carbon monoxide, nitrogen oxide, and nonmethane organic compounds into the atmosphere.

New Uses for Algae Can Help Reduce Carbon Dioxide

Scientists have discovered that algae can help reduce carbon dioxide from the atmosphere. Algae can serve as a substitute for fossil fuels and plastic materials. Algae used in conjunction with AI-powered bioreactors is up to four hundred times more efficient than trees at removing CO2 from the atmosphere. Another plus is that algae grows much faster than trees. Algae can also be used to produce biofuels, which could replace fossil fuels. In a year, algae can produce five thousand gallons of biofuel on a single acre of land (127). Since 1970, scientists have been studying algae as a petroleum substitute. Algae also benefits the environment by replacing plastic materials. Dutch fashion designers Eric Klarenbeek and Maartje Dros are using algae to make polymers for 3-D printing as a replacement for more harmful plastic polymers (127).

BLACK ANGUS, AGATE, UTAH

Dietary Choices Can Drastically Reduce Harmful Greenhouse Gases and Improve Health

Not only does the consumption of red meat negatively impact human health, but it worsens climate change. Cows and fertilizers release methane, which is more harmful than CO2 emissions. If Americans reduced their red meat consumption 40 percent, they could still consume a burger and a half each week while seeing substantial reductions in the amount of methane gas being released into the atmosphere from cattle production (128). Worldwide demand for food is projected to increase by more than 50 percent as personal incomes also increase in developing countries. The demand for red meat products is projected to rise by 75 percent with the projected world population growth (129). Cow, goat, and sheepherding require a lot of land, thus generating more greenhouse gas emissions than growing plants, such as legumes (130). If more people switched to plant-based diets, global emissions would decrease substantially. The entire process of producing meat for human consumption releases as many greenhouse gas emissions as aviation and automobiles combined.

The Mediterranean diet consists of plant-based cooking of fresh local fruits and vegetables, whole grains, beans, seeds, and nuts with chicken and eggs but little red meat. This diet improves longevity and brain function, according to a recent study in the BMJ journal *Gut*. The Mediterranean diet can inhibit the body's production of inflammatory chemicals, which can lead to loss of cognitive function. It can also prevent chronic diseases like diabetes, cancer, and atherosclerosis. These are all reasons why the Mediterranean diet has won first place in the *U.S. News and World Report*'s "best diet" ranking for three consecutive years (131).

More Electric Vehicles Will Help Reduce Harmful Automobile Emissions

By 2030, over 120 million electric vehicles (EVs) are projected to be in use in China, the European Union, and the United States (132). EVs will become more popular as the price of EVs drop and as electric charging stations become more available. The average American spends about $1,300 per year on gasoline combustion vehicles (133). Over a ten-year period, that owner will spend approximately $13,000 on oil and gasoline.

EV purchasers in the United States may qualify for a federal tax credit. According to the IRS, the credit ranges between $2,500 and $7,500, depending on the capacity of the battery and the year of purchase (134). The tax credit serves as an important incentive to buy EVs and hybrids. The federal tax credit is scheduled to phase out over several years unless Congress extends these credits.

Tesla has been the leading producer of electric vehicles. Ford Motor Company has introduced their new Mustang EV. Greenlots and Electrify America are charging companies that will offer the Ford Pass Charging Network access to their charging stations. Both have user-friendly apps that direct drivers to the nearest charging station via smartphone or touch screen. Ford's battery chargers can be used by most electric cars already on the market. Ford's EV customers will also have the option of installing at-home charging stations (135). Researchers have developed a new battery technology that increases the speed at which electric vehicles can be recharged in less than one hour, as opposed to an overnight charge (136). This new technology will make EVs more appealing and convenient for drivers.

Energy-Efficient Homes Can Make a Difference in Fighting Climate Change

Poorly insulated homes and apartment buildings waste significant amounts of energy. The construction and operation of homes and buildings is responsible for nearly 40 percent of the world's greenhouse gas emissions (137). Fortunately, architects and builders are working to make homes and buildings more energy efficient. Structures can now be made to operate so efficiently that they can produce more power than they use. Solar panels and geothermal heat pumps can be installed on most homes and buildings during construction. For residents who cannot afford solar panels, adding insulation in the attic and under floors can reduce heating and cooling bills

(138). Better insulation products now being made from natural materials like wool and cotton, which come from recycled or discarded clothing.

New stick-on solar tiles and solar roof shingles are now available in several colors and styles to match any roof. Sunflare is a company that manufactures solar panels made from stainless-steel substrate with copper, indium, gallium, and selenide to maintain more thinness and flexibility. Tesla is also manufacturing solar tiles for rooftops that carry a lifelong guarantee. Tesla has announced plans to expand its market availability for solar tiles by adding kiosks in stores around the world (139).

Smart thermostats can help reduce the cost of heating and cooling. Many homeowners forget to cut down their thermostats when leaving home. Smart thermostats can be automatically programmed so that heating and cooling systems are operating only when needed. A homeowner can set the smart thermostat using a mobile device (140). Installing blinds or adding curtains can also keep energy costs lower in the summer months.

The Travel and Tourism Industries Are Providing More Earth-Friendly Solutions

Many tourism and travel agencies are taking advantage of Green Globe Certification with specific program recommendations on how to promote environmentally friendly practices at attractions including spas, hotels, golf courses, and ground transportation options. The agencies offer the traveling public and their hosts additional ways to support green practices. Companies that earn Green Globe Certifications are reporting cost savings based on lower water usage (141). Many hotels have eliminated the use of small complimentary plastic bottles included in hotel rooms. This helps reduce the number travel-size toiletry bottles that would otherwise potentially pollute the environment. InterContinental Hotels Group has announced plans to install bulk size dispensers at all its properties by 2021 in their effort to reduce plastic waste. This move will make a significant difference since the company has been distributing about two hundred million travel-size toiletry bottles each year (142). Marriott is following in its footsteps to reduce plastic bottles, which are hard to recycle and take up space in landfills (143).

JetBlue has plans to make all domestic flights carbon neutral starting in July 2020 (144). Heathrow Airport in London has pledged to be carbon neutral by 2030 (145).

Many other businesses are working to reduce carbon emissions to help slow the rate of climate change. Successful businesses that implement carbon reduction into their corporate goals will see increased innovation, competitiveness, risk management, and sales growth (146). But companies should not just be able to say they are carbon neutral. This is called "corporate greenwashing" (147). Company CEOs should be prepared to transparently document their carbon reduction claims.

According to Vox, Natural Capital Partners, an environmental consulting agency, adopted one of the first carbon-neutral guidelines in 2002 for businesses to reach carbon neutrality (148).

The Climate Group's EP100 Initiative helps corporations adopt energy efficiency by bringing together energy-smart companies committed to lowering greenhouse gas emissions and accelerating a clean economy (149).

Massachusetts Has Implemented a Variety of Tax Incentives

Massachusetts has been issuing grants, rebates, and bond programs to encourage consumer investment in energy efficiency. The state leads by example by setting energy requirements for public buildings and auto fleets and benchmarking energy usage (150).

New England States Passed Legislation Called "Bottle Bills," Requiring Glass Bottle Returns

New England led the way decades ago in passing "bottle bills," requiring consumers to return their empty glass bottles to get a return deposit back. Retailers loved this because when some customers failed to return their bottles, they got to keep the deposits (151).

Many recyclers have recently stopped accepting glass bottles for recycling, so perhaps it is time to take a second look at bottle bills as an alternative to trashing all that glass in the landfill.

The Clean Energy DC Omnibus Act

The District of Columbia is adopting one of the most significant climate laws, called the Clean Energy DC Omnibus Act. DC plans to reduce the district's gas emissions by more than 40 percent by encouraging the construction of new energy-efficient buildings by setting a separate minimum energy efficiency standard for each building, to be called the "building energy performance standard." Once the district's energy-efficiency standards have been met, emissions will be cut by almost one million tons per year. DC's plan will spur local investment, job creation, increased attractiveness, and competitiveness for building owners and tenants (153).

Ocean Plastics Charter Plans to Reduce Plastics from Our Oceans

Five of the seven G7 member nations have agreed to an ocean plastics charter, which requires them to work toward making all plastics recyclable by 2030. By reducing single-use plastics and promoting the use of recycled plastics, the member nations to date include France, Italy, Japan, the UK, and Canada (154). Hopefully, the United States and Japan will sign the charter and work with the G7 countries to reduce plastic pollution in the oceans of the world.

Jennifer Morgan, executive director of Greenpeace, observed "governments must move beyond voluntary agreements to legislate binding reduction targets and bans on single-use plastics, invest in new and reuse delivery models for products and hold corporations accountable for the problem they have created" (155). While many countries have expressed an intention to reduce, reuse, and recycle, it is time for all nations to step up and accept responsibility for adopting achievable, measurable, and accountable solutions to reducing plastic waste in our oceans.

Recycling Is Still Necessary to Help Fight Climate Change

In 2017, the United States alone generated 268 million tons of trash. Only about one-third of that total was recycled or composted (156). The rest ended up in landfills or was thrown on roadsides or in rivers, oceans, streams, or lakes. The plastic that was not recycled or put in landfills averaged the equivalent of a hundred plastic bottles per person, according to Jan Dell, an engineer and founder of the Last Beach Cleanup (157). In 2017, only 8.4 percent of all US plastics were recycled (158).

While recycling is still recommended, the recycling industry is struggling to find a profitable market for plastics. China stopped taking recycled plastics in 2018. To make matters worse, there is so much junk mixed in with recyclables that the cost of separating the good recyclables from the unrecyclable plastic bags and Styrofoam items has financially stressed the recycling businesses. Many cities have already cut back on recycling due to their financial losses caused by a weak market for the product (159).

France Is Fighting Inequalities by Protecting Biodiversity and Climate

In 2019, France held a meeting centered around a specific theme of "fighting inequalities by protecting biodiversity and climate." Other G7 members say they are also "committed to the swift and effective implementation of the Paris Agreement and to reaffirm its irreversibility as the essential multilateral framework to address climate change" (160). Several G7 nations also support the Global Climate Action Agenda. Unfortunately, the United States has announced its plans to withdraw from the Paris Agreement in 2020.

USAF Boeing C-17 Globemaster, Charleston, South Carolina

Energy-Efficient Mass Transportation Holds Great Promise for Reducing Climate Change

Developing energy-efficient mass transportation is crucial to addressing climate change. Fuel-efficient airplanes are expected to be in service by 2040. Air travel is responsible for about 2.5 percent of all carbon dioxide emissions. According to projections, the newer, more energy-efficient planes will use 20 percent less fuel (161).

A new study suggests that changing aircraft altitude just two thousand feet could cut a flight's climate impact in half. Scientists at the Imperial College London found that aviation's damage to the climate could be reduced by as much as 59 percent by manipulating where aircraft contrails are released (162). These cloudlike formations have a cooling effect by reflecting sunlight that might otherwise heat up the Earth's atmosphere. A group of MIT scientists concluded that airplane contrails account for 14 percent of air quality damage per unit of aviation fuel burned. Flying the airplane at a slightly higher or lower altitude helps to eliminate airplane contrails. Many countries also have successfully used high-speed rail as an alternative to air travel (163).

An Australian shipping service called Sendle buys carbon credits through the South Pole Group to "cancel out" their carbon emissions since the money goes to sustainability projects (164).

Uber and Lyft are two successful ride-share companies helping people who no longer want the expense of owning a car. However, while a ride-share service is convenient, these two companies are also emitting more pollution. The good news is that both companies are considering switching to electric and hybrid vehicles. Lyft recently bought millions worth of carbon offsets toward becoming a carbon-neutral company. Uber has offered cash rewards for their drivers who agree to use electric vehicles (165).

Distributed Solar Photovoltaics Is Reducing the Harmful Effects of Climate Change

The installation of solar panels is another growing industry that is helping us move to renewable energy as more homes, offices, apartments, and industries are installing solar panels. Solar arrays are now being connected to battery storage so that when the sun is not shining, the stored solar energy can be deployed by utilities to meet peak demand. Long power outages due to storm damage can be mitigated with battery storage and grid resilience. Gas or diesel generators only provide temporary solutions and are expensive to operate (166). By connecting solar panels with battery storage, hospitals, nursing homes, and schools can continue operations.

Utility Scale Solar Photovoltaics Offers the Potential to Transition away from Fossil Fuels

Most investor-owned electric utilities in the United States have either built solar arrays with the approval of state regulators or are purchasing solar energy from large and small solar firms, as required by federal law, because the costs of solar panels has dropped substantially over the years. According to the Bureau of Labor Statistics, the top two fastest-growing occupations are solar photovoltaic installers and wind turbine installers. Jobs in the US solar industry grew by 167 percent during 2019 with an average salary of $42,680 per year (167). Median pay for wind turbine technicians is even more at $54,370, with a 57 percent annual growth rate that same year (168).

Geothermal Represents a Growing Industry Solution for Reducing Global Warming

Geothermal energy uses the Earth's internal heat contained in the rock and fluids beneath the Earth's crust. It can be found in shallow areas to several miles below the surface. Loops can even be submerged under water to capture heat for residential use by installing a geothermal heat pump. The water is circulated through a piping system to take advantage of the constant temperature of the Earth to heat a home during winter months. During the summer months, the heat pump extracts heat from the home or building and transfers it back underground to the relatively cooler ground. This process requires no burning of fossil fuels like oil, gas, or coal. Geothermal energy is always available, and it is 80 percent cheaper compared to burning fossil fuels. It does, however, have some disadvantages because the process releases hydrogen sulfide, a gas that smells like rotten eggs at low concentrations. Some disposal of geothermal fluids, which contain low levels of toxic material, must also be considered. Geothermal fields produce only about one-sixth of the carbon dioxide of a relatively clean natural-gas-fired power plant (169).

Improved Flooding Infrastructure Investments Will Help Mitigate Damages

VIEW FROM PITT STREET BRIDGE, CHARLESTON, SOUTH CAROLINA

Charleston, South Carolina, has been hit hard over the past decade by severe hurricanes, tropical storms and flooding from rising sea levels. The National Weather Service records confirmed there were eighty-nine coastal flooding events along the Southeast coast in 2019 alone (170). Charleston's sea level is projected to rise by six inches by 2040 (171). Charleston broke ground in 2019 for an extended seawall along Charleston's Downtown Low Battery at a cost of $54 million, but some climatologists predict this might only be an effective defense for the next twenty years. Many Charlestonians are understandably shocked by how expensive it will be to protect their homes and businesses from the rising sea levels, causing blue-sky flooding during high tides (172).

WANDO RIVER, CHARLESTON, SOUTH CAROLINA

Climatologists are busy formulating solutions to sea-level rise resulting from global warming and climate change. Many environmental activists have demanded that the fossil fuel industry should help pay for this new infrastructure since state and local governments simply do not have the resources. NASA predicts that global sea level will rise another one to four feet by 2100 as a result of added water from melting land ice and the expansion of seawater as it warms (8).

Georgetown, South Carolina, citizens created a program called "Georgetown RISE," which stands for "resilience, innovation, sustainability, and education" (173). This initiative includes developing a long-term mitigation plan with input from local stakeholders to create a community task force to deal with the adverse impacts of climate change. This local county approach to deal with the destructive impact of climate change holds great promise for other communities to follow.

Eight families living in a cul-de-sac in Baltimore, Maryland, have had to abandon their homes due to repeated flooding making their homes uninhabitable. A grant from the Federal Emergency Management Agency (FEMA) paid for the costs to demolish these homes. More than fifty homes in Maryland have been bought back and demolished using FEMA funds, at a cost of $14 million (174).

Biomass Renewables Are Being Implemented to Increase Energy Efficiency

Biomass plants convert chicken litter, hog waste, and other agricultural and forestry byproducts into electricity and gas. These plants are designed to capture methane gas emissions from decaying waste. Methane is a greenhouse gas that is much more harmful to the environment than carbon dioxide. Renewable energy sources are expected to surpass coal-fired electrical plants that are being retired to reduce carbon dioxide emission levels. Coal-fired capacity retirements in 2018 resulted in 13.5 gigawatts of coal being taken offline. The year 2019 saw another 9.7 gigawatts of coal-fired energy production come offline. More than 20 gigawatts of coal production are expected to come offline by 2024 (175).

Concentrated Solar Energy May Help in the Fight against Climate Change

A recent energy breakthrough called concentrated solar energy holds promise for reducing emissions, especially in the industrial production of steel, cement, and glass. According to CNN Business, concentrated solar energy works by reflecting sunlight off mirrors to produce extreme heat exceeding 1,000°C. According to the International Energy Agency, cement production is responsible for 7 percent of all carbon dioxide emissions. Since steel and cement are both essential building materials for all large infrastructure projects, concentrated solar energy promises to offer substantial reductions in carbon dioxide emissions as it becomes widely available (176).

Bill Gates has reportedly invested heavily in this new technology. Heliogen, a Los Angeles company, is already using concentrated solar to produce cement, steel, and glass (176).

Black Soldier Flies Convert Food Waste into Protein-Reducing Carbon Dioxide Emissions

Black soldier flies eat organic waste, including cafeteria refuse, manure, and toxic algae, turning this into high-quality protein while leaving a smaller carbon footprint. This protein byproduct is being used to feed livestock. Researchers studied the black soldier flies' ability to convert manure into protein as early as 1970 as an efficient way to rapidly process waste (177).

Food waste releases millions of tons of carbon dioxide into the atmosphere, accounting for about 7 percent of the world's greenhouse gas emissions. Louisiana State University uses the black soldier flies to eat leftover cafeteria food. When the flies consume the waste, the carbon and methane that would otherwise have been emitted into the atmosphere is digested. Rotting food is responsible for 7 percent of all greenhouse gas emissions. Using these flies to process rotting food is an efficient way to help the environment and mitigate climate change (178).

Chapter 7

CARBON CAPTURE

Carbon Capture Technology Is Already Being Used to Reduce Global Warming

The growing technology of "carbon capture" could soon be one of the most efficient ways to remove CO_2 out of the atmosphere. "Carbon capture" is a method of capturing and storing CO_2 to slow the rate of global warming and the greenhouse effect. Carbon capture can absorb and store more than 90 percent of emissions that come from power plants. With the developing technologies of carbon capture, emission levels could decline tremendously. The International Energy Agency predicts that carbon capture will be responsible for 14 percent of emission reductions by 2050 (179).

Carbon capture technology separates and traps carbon dioxide, which is then transported by truck or pipeline to a storage site underground. There are three different ways carbon capture can be performed: precombustion carbon capture, postcombustion carbon capture, and oxyfuel carbon capture. The precombustion carbon capture process involves gasifying fuel producing syngas called "synthesis gas," made up of CO and H_2. Precombustion carbon capture can be used with an integrated gasification combined cycle (IGCC) power plant that burns H_2 in a combustion turbine and then uses exhaust to power a steam turbine for power generation. The carbon is captured before the fossil fuel is burned in this process. Postcombustion carbon capture works by using chemical solvents to separate CO_2 out of the flue gas. Postcombustion captures carbon from the fossil fuel once it has already burned. Oxyfuel carbon capture requires that fossil fuel combustion take place in pure oxygen so that the exhaust gas becomes rich with CO2. The carbon is burned by oxygen at the power plant during the oxyfuel capture process. Once carbon is captured, it can be stored underground. Potential underground sites available for carbon dioxide storage are oil and gas reserves, deep saline formations, and abandoned coal beds. The carbon dioxide is injected into these underground sites, where it cannot pollute the air. Carbon capture technology is quite costly, but scientists hope to find ways to reduce the costs as technology advances. Carbon capture has the potential to create hundreds of new high-paying jobs for the world economy (180).

The UN climate scientists estimate that capturing all the Earth's carbon dioxide and sequestering it underground would cost around $300 billion, which is equivalent to the amount the entire world's spends on the military in sixty days (an amount equal to the GDP of Chile) (181).

Carbon can be used to manufacture many products, from soda cans to concrete. Syngas can be turned into jet fuel and plastic. Carbon dioxide can be infused into wet concrete, making it stronger through a process known as "carbon curing." Researchers are finding ways to turn captured carbon into automobile seats, algae biofuels, and building materials (179). George Washington University chemists have discovered a way to transform carbon dioxide into carbon nanofibers, which are used to construct wind turbine blades and manufacture sports equipment (182).

Regenerative Agriculture Reduces Carbon Dioxide and Methane Emissions

Frequent fires and invasive species have hurt farm production and impacted rangelands around the world. In eastern Washington State, invasive weeds in the Channeled Scablands are degrading rangelands and threatening livelihoods for ranchers. The invasive species called medusa's head has emerged as the dominant weed, resulting in a sharp decline in foliage quality, according to Juan Villalba with Utah State University. As pastures degrade, related ecological risks have worsened, including increased risk of wildfires, reduced habitat for wildlife, and the loss of pollinators (183).

The USDA Agricultural Research Service partnered with local ranchers to attack the problem of medusa's head by finding out what other perennial grasses could be planted to improve the resilience of the rangeland. Ranchers found if they let cattle graze on the invasive weed first, it created conditions for planting other healthy perennial grasses. Then, the ranchers could rotate the cattle between the improved areas and the infected areas and then repeat the seeding process. The ranchers saw immediate improvement in their forage production, which has led to stakeholder engagement and program adoption (183).

Commodity growers in the southern United States continue to struggle with controlling certain pests that thrive in warmer weather. Cotton farmers lost over $100 million as a result of these pests between 2008 to 2010. Nematodes cause millions in losses to soybean, peanut, and cotton growers. A Sustainable Agriculture Research and Education (SARE) grant demonstrated that using "interseeding" (planting one crop into a second crop ahead of harvesting the second crop) has the potential to solve some of these concerns. Dan Arco with Clemson University believes interseeding has real potential to demonstrate its efficacy in reducing weed densities and nematode populations (184).

In the semi-arid regions of Nebraska, farmers without irrigation conserve soil water by rotating cereal crops like corn and wheat with a period of summer fallow. Thanks to SARE research, some farmers in the High Plains are finding spring-planted pulse crops to be viable alternatives to summer fallow. Pulse crops consist of legumes like field peas, beans, and chickpeas. Using these pulse crops helps farmers cope with weather and market fluctuations while improving soil health and diversifying crop mix. In 2016, extension educator Strahinja Stepanovic with the University of Nebraska-Lincoln worked with SARE researchers to develop agronomic best practices for growing field peas. Researchers were able to identify the highest-yielding field pea varieties after conducting several trials. This led farmers to adopt an alternative cropping system for corn and soybean rotations. Field peas improved the soil by increasing water infiltration while providing needed habitats for beneficial insects and microorganisms (185).

Indigo Agriculture's goal is to capture one trillion tons of carbon through photosynthesis, one of the most efficient ways to capture carbon. Traditional farming has increased carbon dioxide and methane emissions. Methane, the most harmful greenhouse gas, causes far more intense warming over a much shorter period (187).

COFFEE FARMER, COOPE TARRAZÚ, COSTA RICA

"Regenerative agriculture" includes implementing crop rotation, using cover crops, using fewer chemicals and pesticides, and implementing "no-till" farming and rotational livestock grazing. Indigo Agriculture is encouraging farmers to help sequester carbon emissions by converting their farming operations by using these regenerative techniques (187).

A Carbon Tax Has Been Tried in Several Countries to Reduce Carbon Emissions

Some countries are combating carbon dioxide emissions by adopting a carbon tax on the burning of fossil fuels to make it more expensive for companies to burn fossil fuels. Congress has considered legislation for implementing a carbon tax in the United States, but no action has been taken thus far. Pollution pricing has worked in several countries including Costa Rica and Colombia (187). A similar policy approach was used in the United States to end harmful acid rain ahead of schedule and at a cost cheaper than projected several years ago. Countries that have implemented a carbon tax redistribute the revenue to those most impacted by a tax on fuel. Some leaders support placing a tax on carbon, which would help reduce emission levels without having to rely on expensive sequestration technology that is not yet available at scale.

Electrochemical Plates Might Be Used to Sequester Carbon

MIT engineers have found a new way to sequester carbon out of the air using charged electrochemical plates to absorb carbon. A chemical reaction takes place on the electrochemical plates with a substance called polyanthraquinone, which is composed of carbon nanotubes. The electrodes react with its molecules in the airstream, and the reaction produces a pure form of carbon dioxide. This promising technology could be an excellent way to mitigate climate change (188).

Scientists have found that adding small amounts of marine algae to cattle food can reduce methane emissions from cattle gut microbes by as much as 99 percent (189). California is already seeing reductions in its methane emissions levels.

Carbon Capture Technology Is Currently Costly but Could Become More Affordable

UN climate scientists estimate that if we were able to capture all the Earth's carbon dioxide and sequester it underground, it could cost around $300 billion. That is the equivalent of the GDP of Chile. By returning land to pasture, certain cover crops could convert enough carbon into biomass to stabilize emissions. Sustainable agricultural practices and planting millions of trees could buy us time to ramp up carbon-neutral technologies. There are approximately nine hundred million hectares of vacant land available for restoration. With sustainable land management, sustainable water management, and sustainable soil management, we can make real progress toward reducing future carbon emissions (190).

Clemson University Researchers are Using 3-D Printers and Lasers to Build Electrolyzers

According to the *Greenville Business Magazine*'s February 2019 "Energy Issue," Clemson researcher Joshua Tong is using a $1.6 million grant from the US Department of Energy's Office of Energy Efficiency and Renewable Energy to develop better ways to make hydrogen production easier and more cost effective. This new method of producing clean energy uses electricity to split water into its basic components, oxygen and hydrogen. The hydrogen can then be stored and transported. However, current electrolyzers are cumbersome and require multiple ceramic layers to work properly since each ceramic layer must be heated or "sintered" at differing high temperatures. Tong believes that by using 3-D printers and lasers, he can lower their size and weight by one-tenth; then the more compact units would easily fit into passenger vehicles (191).

Chapter 8:

CLIMATE CHANGE ADVOCATES

European Union President Ursula von der Leyen Has a Plan to Fight Climate Change

The European Union's newest president of the European Commission, Ursula von der Leyen, has plans to make climate change her priority by increasing the EU's emissions reduction target to 55 percent by 2030. Leyen has announced a green deal for Europe in her first one hundred days in office. She proposes that the European Investment Bank serve as a climate bank to unlock a one trillion investment over the next decade. She also supports a carbon tax (192).

Other countries, including Fiji, France, New Zealand, Germany, Portugal, the UK, and Ireland have plans to reduce emissions to zero by 2050. Finland has a goal for zero emissions by 2035. Uruguay and Norway plan to reach a zero-emission goal by as early as 2030. California has set a goal to reach zero emissions by 2045 (193).

In northern England, the education system has included lessons on climate change in the academic agenda. EduCCate Global will help educate teachers on several topics, including climate change science, adaptation planning, health, forests, climate change finance, and international negotiations (194).

The Global Climate Strike in September of 2019 grabbed the attention of the world press. Young climate activists will demonstrate all over the world to mark the fiftieth anniversary of Earth Day on April 22, 2020.

Greta Thunberg Has Inspired a Worldwide Youth Movement

Greta Thunberg, a sixteen-year-old Swedish girl, called upon the world's leaders to fight climate change. She began raising awareness using school protests called "Fridays for Future." Each Friday, Thunberg and her schoolmates would skip class in protest to call attention to the serious impacts of climate change. She dedicated a year of her life, beginning in mid-August of 2019, and sailed the Atlantic from the UK on a boat with solar panels to attend the UN Climate Summit. She refuses to travel via aviation or cruise ship because of its negative effects on global warming. Thunberg has spoken to policymakers at last year's UN Climate Conference in Poland, to business leaders at the World Economic Forum in Davos and to the French and British parliaments. Greta traveled to Rome, where she met with Pope Francis to discuss climate change (196).

Upon her arrival in America, Greta led several strikes with American schoolchildren. Thunberg was invited to the UN on September 23, 2019, where she delivered emotional speech carried live by the media. "You have stolen my dreams and my childhood with your empty words," she implored. "And yet I'm one of the lucky ones. People are suffering. People are dying. Entire ecosystems are collapsing. We are in the beginning of a mass extinction and all you can talk about is money and fairy tales of eternal economic growth" (197).

Thunberg points out that even a 50 percent cut in harmful gas emissions is not enough. Younger generations will spend lifetimes cleaning up the mess that the current generation has made. "You are failing us," she said. "The eyes of all future generations are upon you." Millions have been inspired by Thunberg's courage to stand up and speak out on the issue of climate change (197).

The Women's Earth Alliance Is Educating Young Women about Climate Change

The Women's Earth Alliance works to globally educate and support women and young girls. For thirteen years, the alliance has equipped grassroots women leaders with the skills and tools they need to protect our Earth and strengthen communities from the inside out. The Women's Earth Alliance designs capacity-building trainings where women access skills and tools in appropriate technology, entrepreneurship, and leadership. Educating women and young girls about preventing climate change will empower them to make impactful change.

Every Country Needs a National Climate Change Policy

What is needed is a national climate change policy in every country, which contains specific measurable environmental benefits, including pollution reduction, affordable housing, good jobs, sustainable livelihoods, and community infrastructure. State and local communities must also mobilize their assets toward the development of a just, equitable, and sustainable long-term, comprehensive solution to climate change (199).

Jeff Bezos Commits $10 Billion to Fight Climate Change

On February 17, 2020, Jeff Bezos, CEO of Amazon, announced a $10 billion initiative he calls the Bezos Earth Fund to support environmental scientists, advocates, and organizations working to mitigate the effects of climate change. The fund plans to begin making grants in the summer of 2020. Bezos said that "climate change is the biggest threat to our planet." He said he wanted "to work alongside others both to amplify known ways and to explore new ways of fighting the devastating impact of climate change." Amazon had previously pledged to go carbon neutral by 2040 and plans to deploy one hundred thousand electric delivery vans by 2024 (200).

Chapter 9

CONCLUSION

"The Point of No Return" Is Rapidly Approaching

The year is 2050. Emission levels have not been reduced, and global warming has worsened. The average temperature for a summer day in Columbia, South Carolina, is around 97.7°F. Frederick, Maryland, has become as hot as Tulsa, Oklahoma. New York City no longer has its famous winter with beautiful snow covering the streets because it feels as warm as Virginia Beach. London is as dry as Barcelona, Spain. Seattle feels like San Francisco. Washington, DC, feels like Nashville, Tennessee (201).

Electricity bills are higher than ever before. Heatstroke and air pollution are taking the lives around the world. Much of the world is now too hot to sustain life. Millions have been displaced. This does not have to be our future.

Unless global warming temperatures can be held under 1.5°C over the rest of the twentieth century, 2100 will bring more food insecurity, more droughts, more flooding, more wildfires, more extinct species, and the total abandonment of many coastal cities due to sea-level rise, resulting in millions of displaced people and worsening health outcomes. Countries all over the world must find the political will to adopt immediate initiatives to phase out fossil fuel emissions and transition to clean, renewable energy. The mass transportation sector needs to move rapidly toward electric trucks, trains, and automobiles worldwide. New technologies for battery storage and carbon capture must be pursued aggressively.

In December of 2019, the UN declared that the world is near the "point of no return" if we hope to save the Earth (202). Many nations have failed to meet their voluntary commitments to reduce carbon emissions, as outlined by the Paris Agreement. The UN secretary general has warned that current efforts around the world are inadequate when it comes to seriously addressing this climate crisis. Many central governments around the world simply lack the political will to change. And they never will, unless we all invest our time, our resources, and our collective voices to demand change. There is no Planet B.

Scientist have repeatedly warned us that we only have another decade to reduce harmful emissions to slow the process of global warming, which is worsening the climate crisis. We cannot wait on central governments to act. We must act at the grassroots level. Individuals, small businesses, local communities, towns, cities, states, and large corporations all need to take the climate crisis seriously by changing their behavior and reducing their carbon footprint. We owe it to our children, our grandchildren, and our Planet Earth to act responsibly and to act now.

Let's work to make Earth Day every day!

Ten Ways Governments and Businesses Can Fight Climate Change

1. Set net-zero carbon emissions goals using science-based targets with measurable outcomes like purchasing carbon offsets (203).

2. Congress should renew federal tax credits for individuals and businesses who buy rooftop solar panels and hybrid vehicles, and expand the credits for electric vehicles.

3. Congress should pass a permanent ban on offshore drilling and Arctic drilling.

4. States should not put unreasonable barriers on the installation solar and wind projects.

5. Congress and the states need to support sustainable agricultural practices by using financial incentives for farmers to plant cover crops and use "no-till" farming methods. Farmers around the country are planting cover crops, which protect and improve the soil according to *Cover Crop Economics*, a report published by the USDA (204).

6. Eliminate food waste, as 40 percent of American food goes un-eaten, according to the USDA. The UN estimates that food waste accounts for about 4.4 gigatons of greenhouse gas emissions annually. North America is near the top of the list of food wasters. A Danish company called Too Good To Go is connecting its app users with local restaurants that offer unsold food for one-third of the price. Now, they are expanding to the United States in 2020. In France, Too Good To Go has already signed up over seven thousand business partners who have sold over five million discounted meals according to POLITICO. Bloomberg reports that Food For All, a similar company, has been fighting food waste in New York and Boston since 2016 (205).

7. Construct and maintain more safe walkways, rural bike trails, and city bike lanes.

8. Promote infill commercial and residential development in cities to reduce urban sprawl and cut down on infrastructure expenditures.

9. Expand urban forests, bird sanctuaries, and public parks.

10. Use green refrigerants and appliances to prevent further damage to the ozone layer.

Twenty Things That Individuals Can Do to Fight Climate Change

1. Project Drawdown lists eating a plant-rich diet and reducing food waste as top solutions (206). A 2018 Oxford University study concluded a vegan diet is the single biggest way to reduce greenhouse gases and reduces global acidification, eutrophication, land use, and water use (207).

2. Eat food that is locally grown and in season.

3. Purchase from businesses that align their values with fighting climate change. Eighty-seven percent of customers will likely purchase a product from a company that advocates for an issue they care about (208).

4. Ride a bike, carpool, or take mass transit or walk to work.

5. Buy an electric vehicle.

6. Compost unused food, leaves, and grass clippings (209).

7. Stop using gas-powered leaf blowers, which emit significant greenhouse gases.

8. Cut down on red meat consumption.

9. Avoid airplane flights whenever possible by using teleconference calling.

10. Install rooftop solar panels and solar hot water heaters.

11. Purchase energy-efficient appliances, and lower your water heater temperature.

12. Support and vote for elected officials who are committed to a clean energy future.

13. Avoid investing in the fossil fuel industry or banks that finance fossil fuel projects.

14. Plant native trees and shrubs in your yard, and cut down on pesticide use.

15. Wash clothes in cold water to save energy.

16. Air-dry clothing outside on a clothesline or on an indoor drying rack.

17. Unplug cell phones, laptop chargers, and other appliances when not in use.

18. Use reusable shopping bags rather than plastic bags or paper bags.

19. Reduce, reuse, and recycle (210).

20. Reduce your carbon footprint by choosing to have one less child.

ACKNOWLEDGMENTS

Thank you to my daughter, Graham Ervin, and my son, Matthew Ervin, for allowing me to use their photos.

Thank you to Alexis Rambler for her assistance with background research, writing, and editing.